The Braces Cookbook

Cookbook

Recipes You
(and Your Orthodontist)
Will Love

Pamela Waterman and Brenda Waterman

the Discovery Box
inventive ideas for food, fun & family

Mesa, AZ
www.BracesCookbook.com

Published by the Discovery Box
1955 W. Baseline Rd., Ste. 113-234
Mesa, AZ 85202
www.theDiscoveryBox.com

ISBN-13: 978-0-9774922-0-6
Sixth Printing: February, 2010
Printed in Canada

Dedication

To Jack, Hilary, Gretchen and Jan,
for their patience and collective creativity
as we turned the house into a test kitchen.

Acknowledgments

Thomas A. Tipton, DMD, MDS, Jeffrey D. Wing, DDS, MS, and the orthodontic staff we have come to know and appreciate over the past six years at Tipton and Wing Orthodontics, Tempe, AZ: Beverly, Brenda, DeeDee, Irene, Jeanie, Judy, Michelle, Patty, and Sue — thanks for all your ideas and support

Pamela Burnsworth and Zarina Valente, for their good humor while modeling

The students of the Performing Arts Club (especially Cody Hunt) at Rhodes Jr. High School, Mesa, AZ, for their enthusiastic taste-testing and feedback

The staff at Dobson Montessori Elementary and Junior High School, Mesa, AZ, for helping students learn that cooking is yet another enjoyable life skill

John F. Powers, DMD, Greenbelt, MD

Andrew R. Kious, DDS, MAGD, ABGD, Warner Robins, GA

Douglas Wright, DDS, MS, Amherst, NY

Pam Paladin, American Association of Orthodontists, St. Louis, MO

Cover design by Pam Waterman and 1106 Design, Phoenix, AZ
Interior design by 1106 Design, Phoenix, AZ
Cover photo by Leasures Designer Portraits, Chandler, AZ
Indexing by Shana Milkie, Ann Arbor, MI

— A portion of the proceeds from this book benefits the Smile for a Lifetime Foundation (www.S4L.org), a non-profit group that provides orthodontic scholarships to under-served students.

Contents

* Particularly good for those first few days

* Particularly good for those first few days

* Particularly good for those first few days

Web addresses of orthodontists (with great information and fun
activities), professional organizations, companies with technical
information on types of braces, and people who provide interesting
trivia plus a general history of dentistry and orthodontics

Introduction

Forbidden food? Forget about it! You need *comfort food* for the days when your teeth hurt so much you wonder if you can eat a slice of bread. Whether you have new brackets, elastics, headgear or more, there *are* great foods you can eat — it just takes some thought.

The Braces Cookbook: Recipes You (and Your Orthodontist) Will Love solves this problem by offering 50 different recipes and tips for dishes that are easy on tender teeth yet don't reduce the ingredients to mush. From *Very Tender Vegetables* to *Definitely Deserved Desserts*, each section includes simple directions, substitution specials and orthodontic Tooth Trivia. *Soothing Tips for Difficult Days* helps ease the toughest hours of getting started, *Easy Eating* simplifies packing lunches and fixing quick meals, and *Dining-Out is Do-able* gives suggestions for enjoying restaurant outings and party events. In fact, every aspect of this book helps children, teens, parents and adults readily adapt to life with braces.

Did you just get your wires adjusted? Treat yourself to a *Be-Nice-to-Me Beverage*. Is this the third pair of elastics you're supposed to wear? It's time for a *Mellow Main Meal*. Are you craving "forbidden fruit" (like caramel apples)? Check out the recipe for the Caramel Apple Dip Substitution Special. Enjoy a great mix of luscious tastes, from new twists such as Lime-Graham Cheesecake Nibbles to old favorites like our Best Baked Spaghetti (developed to perfection over 25 years of kitchen crafting.)

Remember, you're not alone. From Chelsea Clinton and Prince Harry to Cameron Diaz and Emma Roberts, more people of all ages are making the most of their smiles and showing them to the world. Flash that trendy smile and indulge yourself in these truly delicious yet braces-friendly delights.

Soothing Tips for Difficult Days

Thousands of braces wearers before you have come up with their own ideas to make this process as comfortable as possible. Try these tips before, during and after.

For you:
- ☐ Take acetaminophen, ibuprofen or your doctor's recommended pain reliever one hour ahead of your appointment. (Students may have to get special permission if this time is during school — be sure to ask first.)
- ☐ Drink or eat something very cold — this delays the movement of your heat-responsive metal wires.
- ☐ Lie down with cold washcloths resting on your cheeks.
- ☐ Rinse your mouth with salt water several times a day.
- ☐ Be sure to keep brushing — just gently, especially after eating sweet desserts.
- ☐ If you're the parent or spouse, keep encouraging your child, teen, husband or wife; if this is for you, pat yourself on the back. Yes, it will hurt for a while for the first couple of days, and each time you have something adjusted, but it's so worth it!

For your cooking:
- ☐ Try microwaving a frozen item instead of popping it in the toaster or oven (think frozen waffles — they definitely come out softer this way).
- ☐ Seal up casseroles and meat dishes with foil while cooking them in the oven — moisture will stay in the dish, and you'll avoid it becoming crispy on the top or edges.
- ☐ Eat leftovers! Many crispy recipes soften up overnight in the refrigerator.
- ☐ Seal freshly baked items in tightly lidded containers — this really helps keep them soft. Or, add a slice of fresh bread to a sealed container of baked goods — the moisture will transfer to the cookies, bars, etc. and soften them up.
- ☐ Use name-brand flour. It really makes a difference in creating fluffier baked goods.

Easy Eating

Brown-bag lunches! Take-out dinners! Fast food! We all need them, so here are suggestions for making simple put-together meals, for home or on the road.

* Items with an asterisk are particularly good for those first Difficult Days.

Main Dish Foods
    American cheese, Brie cheese, Feta cheese
    Burritos, with shredded meat and/or beans
    Chicken — baked, barbequed or in nuggets, cooked until very tender
    Chili*
    Couscous
    Crabmeat, flaked
    Egg salad*
    Fish — boneless, baked, and flaked in small pieces
    Gerber Toddler meat sticks/turkey sticks/chicken sticks (they come in a jar)*
    Grilled cheese sandwiches, with crusts cut off
    Hormel Vienna sausages (in a can)
    Hot dogs, boiled and cut up
    Macaroni & cheese, well cooked*
    Meatloaf — very moist, with lots of breadcrumbs in it
    Pasta — any kind, well cooked, with sauce*
    Pot stickers (Chinese dumplings)
    Ramen noodles*
    Ravioli — canned or well cooked from frozen*
    Rice — plain or flavored
    Salmon — baked or poached
    Soups*
    Tacos — soft
    Taquito roll-ups — microwaved, so they don't get crunchy
    Tamales, canned
    Tortellini, well cooked
    Tuna salad
    Yogurt*

Breakfasts
Cream of Wheat hot cereal*
Eggs — boiled, scrambled, poached
Oatmeal hot cereal*
Pancakes
Waffles

Vegetables/Fruit
Acorn squash* — baked
Apples — cut into thin slices
Applesauce*
Bananas — ripe
Carrots — boiled
Corn — cooked on the cob, but cut off with a knife
Grapefruit — ripe
Grapes — cut in half
Guacamole dip on pita bread slices
Mandarin orange slices
Pears — ripe or canned slices
Pear sauce, or any of the other new fruit mixtures*
Potatoes — baked, mashed*

Desserts
Cream pies
Ice cream, frozen yogurt, popsicles and sherbet (without nuts or
    candy chunks)*
Jello*
Pudding — made from a box, or in individual pudding cups*
Tapioca pudding*

Beverages
Fruit juice
Milkshakes*
Smoothies (fruit, yogurt, ice cream, etc.)*
Tomato juice

Dining-Out is Do-Able

Think you're stuck at home with your braces, or doomed to carry a sack lunch everywhere? With a little creativity, your away-from-home eating can still be delicious and safe for your braces. Read on for do-able ideas.

In restaurants:

Tamales instead of tacos

Corned beef hash instead of steak, roast or pork

Sloppy Joes instead of hamburgers

Lasagna instead of pizza

Noodle dishes instead of thick pasta; you may be able to order them "well done"

Cooked vegetables instead of raw ones

Baked or mashed potatoes instead of French fries

Baked or steamed fish instead of fried fish

At parties:

Instead of eating hard crackers with a dip, see if there are bread slices and spread the dip with a spoon or small knife

Try potato chips instead of tortilla chips

Ask for a fork and knife to cut finger food into individual bites

Give yourself permission to leave the crusts from pizza and sandwiches

Be-Nice-to-Me
Beverages ▶▶▶

▼ ▼ ▼

Mmm Mmm Milk Shakes

Chocolate
1 cup milk
2 Tablespoons light cream
1 Tablespoon chocolate syrup
¼ cup chocolate ice cream
¼ cup vanilla ice cream

Vanilla
1 cup milk
2 Tablespoons light cream
½ teaspoon vanilla extract
½ cup vanilla ice cream

Mix all ingredients in a blender or stir very well by hand. Makes one serving.

▼ ▼ ▼

Flavored Ice-Cream Shakes

Coffee or Mocha
1¼ cups ginger ale
1 cup coffee ice cream
2 teaspoons instant coffee
  granules *or* 1 Tablespoon
  chocolate syrup

Black Cow
1¼ cups root beer
1 cup vanilla ice cream
¼ teaspoon vanilla extract

Strawberry
1¼ cups ginger ale
1 cup strawberry ice cream
(optional: ½ cup cut-up
  strawberries)

Chocolate
1¼ cups cola
1 cup chocolate ice cream
1 Tablespoon chocolate syrup

Mix all ingredients in a blender or stir very well by hand. Makes one serving.

▲▲▲▲▲▲▲▲▲▲▲▲▲▲▲▲▲▲▲▲▲▲▲▲▲▲▲▲▲▲▲▲▲▲▲▲

▼ ▼ ▼

Fabulous Fruit Smoothies

For a quick, soothing breakfast or afternoon snack, put together the ingredients ahead of time. Keep the mixture in the refrigerator ready to whip together in a blender.

_____

> 2 bananas
> 1 cup milk
> 1 cup other fruit (raspberries, blueberries, strawberries,
>   mandarin oranges, etc., fresh or thawed from frozen)
> (optional: 2 Tablespoons protein powder)

Cut bananas into 1-inch slices. Add all ingredients to a blender, and mix for 10 seconds on a low setting. Makes two servings.

▼ ▼ ▼

Yummy Yogurt Smoothies

This yogurt variation on the previous recipe was a terrific hit at a Scouting event that attracted more than a hundred thirsty taste-testers. You could substitute strawberries, blueberries or whatever fruit is in season.

_____

> 1 banana
> 1 cup raspberries (fresh or thawed)
> ⅓ cup non-fat vanilla yogurt
> ½ cup apple juice

Cut up the banana in 1-inch slices. Add all ingredients in a blender, and mix for 15 seconds on a low setting. Makes one serving.

▲▲

▼ ▼ ▼

Cranberry Splash Punch

This was a favorite summer refresher and party beverage when I was in college, and it still hits the spot when you need a little sparkle!

----

1 (2-liter) bottle ginger ale (chilled)
1 (64-oz.) bottle cranberry juice (chilled)
2 Tablespoons lemon juice
Ice cubes
(optional: lime slices)

In a large punch bowl, combine ginger ale, cranberry juice and lemon juice. Stir well. Add a dozen or more ice cubes to keep the punch chilled, and optional lime slices for decoration. Serves 12–16.

For a variation, try cranberry-raspberry, cranberry-grape, or cranberry-cherry juice.

Tooth Trivia...

Braces in the '60s used stainless steel wires
that needed frequent tightenings and shifts.
Nowadays, orthodontists use nickel-titanium
alloy wires developed by NASA. This lightweight
wire becomes "active" as it warms to body
temperature, gradually moving the teeth
in the direction desired.

▲▲▲

Bracket-Friendly
Breads and Breakfasts ▶▶▶

▼ ▼ ▼

Banana Bread

In our house, this banana bread always disappears in less than 24 hours — it's a treat for breakfast, lunch and snacks, and breaks easily into tiny bites for tender-teeth days. When your braces come off, you could add half a cup of chopped walnuts.

---

3 large or 4 small ripe bananas, sliced
½ cup (1 stick) margarine (allow to soften an hour at
    room temperature if you have time)
1 cup sugar
2 eggs
2 cups all-purpose flour
1 teaspoon baking soda
½ teaspoon salt

Preheat oven to 350 degrees. Bake for 60–65 minutes.

In a small bowl, use an electric mixer to blend the bananas together; set them aside. In a large bowl, cream the margarine, sugar and eggs. Add the flour, soda and salt to the egg mixture, then add the bananas. The batter will be a bit stiff.

Grease a 9"x5" loaf pan with shortening or spray-oil, then pour in batter. Bake at 350 degrees for 60 to 65 minutes, depending on how dark you like the crust. It cuts into neater slices if you let it cool for half an hour, but we can never wait!

Tooth Trivia...
The word "malocclusion," the mismatch of your
top teeth meeting your bottom teeth, comes from
the Latin words for "bad bite."

▲▲

▼ ▼ ▼
Zucchini Bread

Somehow I feel very healthy eating this bread. It's one of my children's favorites, and since it makes two loaves, it's a great idea to keep one in the freezer for a quick morning treat. You can grate zucchini ahead of time (when your neighbors load you up on free produce from a garden gone crazy) and freeze it in bags of two cups each. Just thaw it in the fridge before using.

1¾ cups sugar
3 eggs
¾ cup vegetable oil
2 cups peeled, finely grated zucchini
1½ teaspoons vanilla
3 cups all-purpose flour
1½ teaspoons salt
1 teaspoon baking soda
¼ teaspoon baking powder
1 teaspoon cinnamon

Preheat oven to 325 degrees. Bake for 1 hour and 10 minutes.

In a large bowl with an electric mixer, combine all ingredients. (Don't you love this kind of recipe?) Grease two 9"x5" loaf pans and pour in batter. Bake at 325 degrees for 1 hour and 10 minutes.

Tooth Trivia...
On the PBS TV show <u>Zoom</u>, Keiko had full metal bands.
They even filmed a segment about getting them put on.

▲▲▲▲▲▲▲▲▲▲▲▲▲▲▲▲▲▲▲▲▲▲▲▲▲▲▲▲▲▲▲▲▲▲▲▲▲▲▲

▼▼▼

Scrumptious Scones
(Raisin or Chocolate)

This cross between a muffin and a cookie is soft, light and fluffy (the secret is cream of tartar) — nothing like the dry rocks that some shops pass off as scones. The recipe came directly from a friend in Devonshire, England more than 40 years ago; the only possible improvement came from Daughter #2, Gretchen, who came up with the chocolate version below.

———————

1½ cups raisins (soak them ahead of time in a cup of
    hot tap water, at least ten minutes, then drain)
2¾ cups all-purpose flour
4 Tablespoons margarine, not butter (softened at room
    temperature if you have time)
¼ cup sugar
2 teaspoons baking soda
4 teaspoons cream of tartar
¼ teaspoon salt
1 cup milk
small amount of flour for cutting board

Preheat oven to 450 degrees. Bake for 9 minutes.

Presoak raisins. In a large bowl, use a fork or a pastry chopper to mix the flour and margarine. With a large spoon, mix the remaining ingredients except raisins and milk. Drain the raisins and stir them in. Stir in milk. Dough will be soft, sticky and fluffy.

On a large, well-floured cutting board, gently spread the dough into a rectangle approximately 9" x 12." Dip a knife into flour to keep dough from sticking to it, and cut the dough into 8 squares. Cut the squares again on the diagonal to make 16 triangular scones. Using a floured spatula, transfer the scones to an ungreased cookie sheet. Bake at 450 degrees for 9 minutes. They will be golden brown on top.

Wonderful when eaten warm, these scones also freeze perfectly and can be easily reheated (wrapped in a damp paper towel) in a microwave. Try 45 seconds on half-power.

Chocolate variation from braces-veteran Gretchen Waterman: add an additional ¼ cup of sugar, and replace the raisins with 12 oz. of chocolate chips. Bake just 8 minutes. Better for you than traditional chocolate chip cookies!!

▲▲▲▲▲▲▲▲▲▲▲▲▲▲▲▲▲▲▲▲▲▲▲▲▲▲▲▲▲▲▲▲▲▲▲▲▲▲

▼ ▼ ▼
Perfect Pancakes

As much as I love going out for breakfast, I have to confess I rarely order pancakes — no restaurant version has ever met the standards set by this simple family recipe. When you let the batter rest for five to ten minutes before cooking, it guarantees classic fluffiness, and isn't that what pancakes are all about? For fun, try making them "silver dollar size."

Preheat a flat griddle (non-stick or greased) to medium-high to start; it's ready when water droplets dance on the surface. Lower the temperature to produce just the shade of golden tan that your family prefers.

> 2 cups all-purpose flour
> 3 teaspoons baking powder
> ½ teaspoon salt
> 2 eggs
> 1¾ cups milk
> 4 Tablespoons vegetable oil

In a large bowl, whisk (or use electric mixer on low) together all ingredients. Let batter sit for five to ten minutes to activate the baking powder.

Scoop up about ⅓ cup batter and pour it onto the griddle; make four or five pancakes at a time. When bubbles start to appear on the tops, flip them over and brown the other side. Makes about 14 5-inch pancakes.

Variation: Use one cup white flour plus one cup whole-wheat flour.

Low on syrup? Make your own by boiling until sugar melts:

> 1 cup brown sugar
> ⅓ cup water
> Dash of salt
> Drop of vanilla extract

▼▼▼
Wonderful Waffles

Forget the recipe that came with your waffle iron — this is the one for fluffy, melt-in-your-mouthness. The secret is letting the batter "rest" for five minutes before using. Top with syrup, jam, fresh fruit or even ice cream.

Preheat your waffle iron according to the directions. You may want to lightly spray it with vegetable oil before heating.

> 3 cups all-purpose flour
> 2 Tablespoons + 2 teaspoons baking powder
> 1 teaspoon salt
> 2 Tablespoons sugar
> 4 cups milk
> 4 eggs
> ½ cup vegetable oil

In a large bowl, whisk (or use electric mixer on low) together all ingredients. Let batter sit for about five minutes to activate the baking powder.

When waffle iron is ready to use, pour about ⅓ cup of batter onto each of the four squares (experiment with your iron — you don't want the batter overflowing.) Gently close the cover and set your timer as the manufacturer suggests. Do not lift the cover while they bake. When done, carefully lift one edge with a flat spatula and pull the waffle away from the iron. Keep waffles warm on a plate under a clean dishtowel while the others bake. Makes about five of the four-square style of waffles.

This recipe works well cut in half for a smaller batch.

Tooth Trivia...
If you are right-handed, you probably chew most of the time with the teeth on the right side of your mouth.

▲▲

▼ ▼ ▼

David Eyre (or Baby Dutch) Pancakes

Go for the "wow" effect with this lighter-than-air, oven-baked confection. One pancake makes four large slices; we always pop a second one into the oven to bake while we sit down to eat the first one. Traditionally, one sprinkles lemon juice and powdered sugar on top, but you could also try various jams, applesauce or cut-up fruit. Eat them while they're hot!

Per pancake:
2 Tablespoons margarine
2 eggs
½ cup milk
½ cup all-purpose flour
Pinch of salt
⅛ teaspoon nutmeg

lemon juice (served in a small pitcher)
powdered sugar (served in a small bowl)

Preheat oven to 425 degrees. Bake for 20 minutes.

Place the margarine in a 9" or 10" pie pan, and put the pan in the oven just long enough to melt the margarine (check at one minute.) Swirl the margarine so that it coats the bottom and sides of the pan.

In a large bowl, with a mixer or whisk, combine the eggs, milk, salt, and whatever margarine you can pour out of the pan, until frothy. Beat in flour and nutmeg; leaving some lumps is fine. Pour mixture into coated pie pan. Bake at 425 degrees for 20 minutes. Serve as soon as possible so everyone sees the beautiful puff!

▼ ▼ ▼

Apple (Not Too) Crisp

Fall, Winter, Spring, Summer: enjoy the tang of an apple without the crunch. The fine crumb topping on this tender cinnamon-y dessert will stay soft if you cover the baking dish with foil as soon as it comes out of the oven.

---

  4 cups (about 8 large apples) peeled, coarsely sliced
  apples (MacIntosh and Rome apples work well; avoid
  Delicious apples)
  ¼ cup water
  1 teaspoon cinnamon
  ¾ cup all-purpose flour
  ¾ cup sugar
  ⅓ cup margarine, chopped into small bits

Preheat oven to 350 degrees. Bake for 35 to 40 minutes.

In a 9"x13" pan, or a 2-quart casserole, spread the sliced apples. Sprinkle with the water and cinnamon.

In a small bowl, combine flour, sugar and margarine with a pastry cutter or fork, until mixture becomes fine crumbs. Sprinkle crumb topping over apples. Bake at 350 degrees for 35 to 40 minutes, depending on how dark you like the crumbs.

Cover with foil while warm to soften the topping. Makes eight servings. Goes well with a scoop of vanilla ice cream on top.

Tooth Trivia...
Around 400 B.C. in Greece, the great medical scientist and writer Hippocrates wrote of attempts to straighten teeth.

▲▲▲

▼ ▼ ▼

Lemon Pudding-Cake

Reminiscent of a fruit cobbler, this fragrant casserole dish makes an unusual breakfast accompaniment, especially warm out of the oven. You've had lemon Danish, so why not Lemon Pudding-Cake?

---

1 cup sugar
¼ teaspoon salt
3 Tablespoons lemon juice
3 eggs, separated
⅓ cup all-purpose flour
2 Tablespoons margarine (melted)
1½ cups milk
hot water

Preheat oven to 325 degrees. Bake for 55 to 60 minutes.

Grease a 2-quart casserole, then find a pan that is large enough to hold the casserole with room for an inch of water.

In a large bowl, with a whisk or electric mixer, combine sugar, salt, lemon juice and egg yolks. Add flour, mixing well, then stir in melted margarine and milk.

In a small bowl, with an electric mixer, beat egg whites until stiff. Fold them into the lemon mixture. Pour batter into casserole (the batter may be a bit lumpy), then place the casserole in the larger pan. Pour hot water to about the one-inch level around the casserole. Bake pudding-cake at 325 degrees for 55 to 60 minutes, until the cake is golden and the bottom layer is a semi-firm pudding texture. Be careful taking the pan out of the oven — the water is very hot and makes the double pan heavy.

Makes four to six servings. Great hot or cold.

▼ ▼ ▼

Twisty Soft Pretzels

Just like the ones you pay two dollars for at the mall kiosks, these are big and soft. Get them while they're hot!

¾ cup warm water
½ envelope yeast
1 teaspoon sugar
2 cups all-purpose flour
½ teaspoon salt
1 egg, beaten
Pinches of salt or cinnamon-sugar

Preheat oven to 425 degrees. Bake for 12 minutes.

In a small bowl, stir together warm water, yeast and sugar. In a large bowl, mix salt and flour with a large spoon. After 5 minutes, stir yeast mix into flour mix.

With well-floured hands, shape dough into 6-inch rods, initials, animals or traditional twisted pretzel shapes. Brush them with the beaten egg and place on a greased cookie sheet. If desired, sprinkle them with extra salt or cinnamon-sugar. Bake at 425 degrees for 12 minutes.

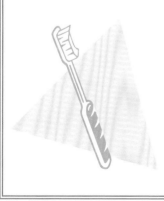

Tooth Trivia...

Some orthodontics have gone wireless!
A new, almost invisible style of braces uses a
series of 18 to 30 individual, removable,
successive plastic "sleeves" that slide over the
teeth and gently nudge them into new places.
Each sleeve is worn for two weeks — and the
world may never know you're wearing them.

▲▲▲▲▲▲▲▲▲▲▲▲▲▲▲▲▲▲▲▲▲▲▲▲▲▲▲▲▲▲▲▲▲▲▲▲▲▲▲

Mellow
Main Meals ▶▶▶

▼▼▼

Meatballs in Herbed Tomato Sauce

You might not think that meatballs could "bake" in a pot full of sauce, but that's just the ticket to making these melt-in-your-mouth temptations. Serve with a side of Very Tender Vegetables, and you have a Mellow Main Meal that everyone will enjoy.

———————

1 pound ground beef
¼ cup uncooked long-grain rice
1 beaten egg
2 Tablespoons ketchup
2 teaspoons parsley
⅛ teaspoon chopped garlic
½ teaspoon salt
1 Tablespoon dried onion or ¼ cup chopped onion
1 (10¾ oz.) can undiluted tomato soup
½ cup water
1 teaspoon Worcestershire sauce

In a large bowl, mix together beef, rice, egg, ketchup, parsley, garlic, salt and onion. Shape into 1-inch balls; this takes about 10 minutes.

In a Dutch oven pot, stir together tomato soup, water and Worcestershire sauce; add meatballs and put on stove on medium-high. Bring sauce to a boil, then turn down until just bubbling. Cover and simmer about 35 minutes; stir sauce and meatballs halfway through to keep them from sticking. Check that no pink shows in a cut-open meatball. Makes about 30 meatballs, serving five to six; this recipe doubles well.

Tooth Trivia...
In the movie The Princess Diaries, Mia (Anne Hathaway) pops in a retainer while arguing with her mother about finding out she's an unlikely princess.

▲▲

▼ ▼ ▼
Best Baked Spaghetti

The first time I was served this casserole, I unashamedly had three helpings. The Burgundy makes it rich and mellow, while the oregano contributes fragrance and flavor. You can divide the cheese as you like, to put more throughout or on top — we love the browned-yet-tender topping that it forms. This freezes well, and the leftovers are great, too.

---

1 pound ground beef
1 medium onion, chopped *or* 1 tablespoon dried onion
1 clove garlic, chopped
3 (8 oz.) cans tomato sauce
½ cup Burgundy or merlot wine (Burgundy gives a
    deeper flavor)
1 teaspoon dried oregano
(optional: ½ teaspoon dried parsley)
1 tablespoon sugar
½ teaspoon salt
½ cup grated American cheese, about 4 slices, or ½ cup
    grated mild cheddar cheese
½ pound dry spaghetti, broken in half

Preheat oven to 350 degrees. Baking time 45 minutes.

In a large no-stick frying pan or Dutch oven, sauté meat, onion and garlic. Add tomato sauce, wine, oregano, parsley, sugar and salt. Simmer, covered, 1 hour, stirring occasionally. (It really makes a difference if you can take this amount of time! Otherwise, 20 minutes will serve to heat everything.)

Cook spaghetti and drain. Put half the spaghetti in a greased 3-quart casserole, then add half the sauce and ¼ cup of the grated cheese. Add the remaining spaghetti and sauce, and stir everything together with a large spoon. Sprinkle the remaining cheese on top.

At this point, the ingredients are all cooked, so it could be eaten as is, but it's much better if you bake it (covered) at 350 degrees for 45 minutes — the cheese turns a wonderful brown and the flavor is absorbed throughout. Serves six to eight.

▼▼▼
Creamy Tuna Noodle Casserole

This was comfort food when I was growing up, and continues to be a quick solution for tender-teeth days. Personalize it with your choice of topping: crumbled Ritz crackers or Saltines, bread crumbs mixed with a few tablespoons of parmesan cheese, or, the classic favorite — crushed potato chips!

2½ cups medium or wide egg noodles
Water for boiling noodles
2 (7 oz.) cans tuna (drained and flaked apart)
2 (10¾ oz.) cans undiluted cream of chicken or cream
    of mushroom soup
⅔ cup milk
½ cup of your choice: crushed Ritz or Saltine crackers,
    potato chips, or bread crumbs (with 1 Tablespoon
    grated Parmesan cheese)

Preheat oven to 350 degrees. Bake for 40 minutes, covered.

In a large pot, boil water and cook noodles until not quite tender. Grease a 2-quart casserole and stir in the noodles, tuna and soup. Pour milk over noodle mixture. Sprinkle with the crackers, chips or crumb mixture. Cover and bake for 40 minutes at 350 degrees. Serves six.

Tooth Trivia...
On the <u>Cosby</u> TV show, Denise had real braces
during the first season.

▼ ▼ ▼

Tender Chicken Pot Pie

This dinner pie is one of the best reasons to have cut-up cooked chicken on hand in the freezer. Ditto for bags of frozen chopped broccoli and frozen potato "shreds." Add canned soups, refrigerator crescent rolls and a few seasonings, and you won't want to go back to those ordinary meat pies again.

———

1 (10¾ oz.) can undiluted cream of celery soup
1 (10¾ oz.) can undiluted cream of chicken soup
¾ cup milk
¼ teaspoon thyme
2 cups chopped frozen broccoli (thawed)
2 cups cut-up cooked chicken
2 cups shredded frozen potatoes (thawed)
1 cup cooked carrots (fresh is best, rather than frozen)
2 (8 oz.) cans refrigerated crescent rolls (8 per can)

Preheat oven to 400 degrees. Bake for 30 minutes total.

In a 9" x 13" pan, stir together the two cans of soup, milk, and thyme. Stir in the broccoli, chicken, potatoes and carrots.

Bake the pan uncovered at 400 degrees for 15 minutes only. Remove the pan from oven but leave the oven on.

Unroll both cans of crescent rolls, and divide each can into four rectangular sections (don't break them into triangles.) Lay all the rectangles across the top of the chicken mixture, overlapping as necessary to fit.

Bake pan at 400 degrees for another 15 minutes, until rolls are nicely golden. Makes 10 to 12 servings.

▼▼▼

Simmered Soy Chicken Wraps

Whether you use a slow-cooker or a Dutch oven, the longer this filling simmers, the more melt-in-your-mouth tender it becomes. This seasoned, shredded chicken wraps up to perfection in soft tortillas — we love to use whole wheat type for extra flavor.

---

3 boneless chicken breast halves
2 large onions, chunked
Small flour tortillas (pkg. of ten), wheat or white
(optional: 10 to 16 oz. of cooked chopped broccoli)

Sauce:
¼ cup soy sauce
¼ cup water
2 Tablespoons honey
⅛ teaspoon ginger
2 Tablespoons peach or apricot jam
1 Tablespoon cornstarch

In a slow cooker, or a large pot on the stove, layer the onions and the chicken breasts. Allow at least three hours in the slow cooker on medium, or at least one hour on the stove — the longer the better, but you don't have to do anything to it while it cooks.

Spoon out the chicken onto a cutting board, and with a knife and fork, shred the chicken as finely as you'd like. In a small saucepan, stir all sauce ingredients together over medium heat until the mixture starts bubbling, then let it simmer for five minutes on low heat to thicken.

In a serving bowl, stir sauce and onions into chicken; if you'd like, add cooked chopped broccoli. Let your guests spoon the mixture into their own tortillas and wrap them up; eating by hand is encouraged! Serves six to eight.

▲▲▲▲▲▲▲▲▲▲▲▲▲▲▲▲▲▲▲▲▲▲▲▲▲▲▲▲▲▲▲▲▲▲▲▲▲▲▲

▼ ▼ ▼

Moroccan Sweet-Pepper Chicken

This is a wonderfully tender stir-fry to serve with white or brown rice. It may convince you to keep diced peppers (green, red, yellow and orange) in your freezer for spur-of-the-moment use. The sauce also uses "from the cupboard" ingredients, though if you're out of sherry, don't worry — it will still be very tasty.

---

3 boneless chicken breast halves, boiled
3 cups (fresh or frozen, unthawed) sweet peppers, diced
   (any color)

Sauce:
$\frac{1}{3}$ cup orange juice
$\frac{1}{4}$ cup soy sauce
$\frac{1}{4}$ teaspoon ginger
1 Tablespoon sherry
1 Tablespoon vinegar
1 Tablespoon cornstarch
(optional: $\frac{1}{4}$ cup sliced almonds)

In a large pot, boil the chicken breasts until very tender, about 1 hour. (This is a great task to do ahead of time while getting other things done in your life.) Shred the chicken on a cutting board and set aside.

In a Dutch oven or large covered frying pan, simmer the peppers in $\frac{1}{2}$ cup water for 15 minutes. Add shredded chicken and keep on low heat.

In a small bowl, use a whisk to stir together all the sauce ingredients except the almonds. Pour the sauce over the chicken and pepper mixture and simmer the combination, covered, for ten minutes.

Serve over rice and, if desired, add the almonds on top for non-braces eaters. Makes six to eight servings.

▼ ▼ ▼

Three-Cheese Macaroni Extravaganza

This is "the real thing" that those boxed versions try to imitate, and keeping packages of pre-shredded cheeses on hand make it almost as quick to prepare. You can boil the macaroni noodles to your preferred level of tenderness, and let the blended flavors of the three real cheeses elevate this dish to gourmet cuisine. Zip it up with onion, or keep the Tabasco sauce handy for the really adventurous — but enjoy its natural simplicity.

_____

2 cups uncooked macaroni noodles
Water for boiling
(optional: 1 or 2 onions, chopped)
(optional: 1 to 2 Tablespoons margarine for sautéing
    onions)
½ cup grated Parmesan cheese (fresh is best, but the
    canned type works too)
½ cup shredded Mozzarella cheese
½ cup shredded mild or sharp cheddar cheese
1½ cups milk
½ cup bread crumbs or dry stove-top stuffing

Preheat oven to 350 degrees. Bake for 40 minutes.

In a medium pot, boil macaroni in water until you can just cut it with the side of a fork; drain and set aside. In a medium saucepan, sauté the onions in the margarine until they are clear and tender.

In a 3-quart greased casserole, stir together the macaroni and milk. Sprinkle with the cheeses and onion, then stir it all together. Sprinkle the bread crumbs on top.

Cover and bake for 40 minutes at 350 degrees. Serves six to eight.

▲▲▲▲▲▲▲▲▲▲▲▲▲▲▲▲▲▲▲▲▲▲▲▲▲▲▲▲▲▲▲▲▲▲▲▲▲

▼ ▼ ▼

Baked Ham n' Egg Hash-Browns

A great make-ahead casserole, this dish really simplifies life. Mix it the night before, then pop it in the oven for a quick dinner after an orthodontist's appointment! Instead of the chopped ham, try using deli ham for maximum tenderness, and shred it yourself with a kitchen shears.

---

3 cups frozen shredded hash-brown potatoes, uncooked
¾ cup shredded Monterey Jack or cheddar cheese (you
    choose, mild or sharp)
1 cup diced cooked ham or shredded deli ham
4 eggs, beaten
1 (12 oz.) can evaporated milk
⅛ teaspoon salt

Preheat oven to 350 degrees. Bake for 40–45 minutes (or 55–60 minutes if made ahead and chilled).

Grease a 2-quart casserole. Spoon shredded potatoes on the bottom, then top with the cheese and ham. In a large bowl, whisk together the eggs, evaporated milk and salt. Pour egg mixture over ham mixture in casserole.

Bake for 40–45 minutes at 350 degrees; if chilled, bake 55–60 minutes. Let stand for five minutes before serving. Serves six.

Tooth Trivia...

Dr. Edward Angle (1855–1930) is considered by some as "The Father of Modern Orthodontics." In the 1890s, he was one of the first dentists to consider the importance of how your teeth come together to form your "bite." He founded the world's first school for orthodontic education in St. Louis Missouri in 1899.

▼▼▼

Soft-Crust Pizza

Fast, easy, and fun for children to do themselves or as a family "assembly project," these pizzas make use of pre-mixed biscuit dough. Don't have any on hand? See the mix-it-yourself directions below, then let your imagination lead you to new possibilities in pizza perfection. You might want to make two!

---

1 Tablespoon corn meal
3 cups biscuit mix (purchased, or from below)
1½ cups water
Spray-type vegetable oil, or vegetable oil with a brush
2 to 3 cups pizza sauce (purchased)
1 to 1½ cups of grated cheeses (mozzarella, Asiago,
   mild Cheddar, Parmesan)
Your choice of green peppers, sausage or bacon (cooked
   and crumbled), pepperoni slices, mushrooms, etc.,
   chopped in small pieces

Preheat oven to 450 degrees. Pre-bake crust for 4 minutes, then bake complete pizza for 13 minutes.

Sprinkle corn meal all over a cookie sheet or pizza pan. In a large bowl, with a spoon, stir together the biscuit mix and the water. Sprinkle your hands with flour, then pat the dough into a 12-inch circle or square, directly on the pan. Build up a bit of dough around the edge to make a rim for holding in the sauce. Spray or brush the dough lightly with oil, then bake for just 4 minutes at 450 degrees.

Carefully pour pizza sauce on top, then add grated cheese and the other toppings of your choice. Bake complete pizza for an additional 13 minutes at 450 degrees, checking that the edges are just golden, to keep them soft.

Biscuit Mix:
3 cups all-purpose flour
½ cup nonfat dry powdered milk
2 Tablespoons baking powder
½ teaspoon salt
½ cup shortening

In a large bowl, combine all ingredients with a pastry cutter or fork. Makes a generous 3 cups of biscuit mix. Keep any extra mix refrigerated in a sealed bowl or bag; it will keep for a few weeks. (See Crustless Quiche, p. 46, for another recipe using this mix.)

▲▲

▼▼▼
Crustless Quiche

Never again will the task of making piecrust stop you from enjoying classic quiche. This super quick recipe combines just six ingredients all mixed together, yet it produces a beautifully sliceable egg and cheese quiche. Pre-shredded cheese and a packaged biscuit mix make it extra easy but very light.

---

3 eggs
½ cup packaged biscuit mix (or make your own — see
   recipe on p. 45)
3 Tablespoons vegetable oil
1½ cups milk
1½ cups shredded Swiss cheese
1 (6 oz.) can crab meat, drained and flaked apart

Preheat oven to 350 degrees. Bake for 50 minutes.

Grease or spray a 10" pie pan or quiche dish. In a large bowl, with a whisk, beat the eggs, biscuit mix, vegetable oil and milk. Pour mixture into pan; it will be lumpy. Sprinkle on the cheese and crab meat. Bake for 50 minutes at 350 degrees. Let stand 10 minutes before cutting.

A nice variation substitutes mild Cheddar cheese for the Swiss, and bacon bits or shredded deli ham for the crab. Both versions freeze well. Serves six to eight.

Tooth Trivia...
As recently as the 1960s, it could take all day
to put braces on a patient.

Shredded Jerky Jumbles

Brenda really misses gnawing on a strip of beef jerky, so this became the challenge as one of our first Substitution Specials. It's quite easy, but makes all the difference for tender teeth.

---

2 ounces dried beef jerky, any flavor
1 cup boiling water

Cut the beef jerky into quarter-inch bits with a kitchen shears or sharp knife. Put them in a large bowl, and pour the boiling water over them. Let the jerky bits soak for 30 minutes, then drain off the water. Eat them with a spoon — hurray!

Tooth Trivia...

If you ever have to have a root canal, the wonders of anesthetics make it just another dental procedure. And while you're in the chair, think about this: the material the endodontist uses as filler is "gutta-percha" — originally used by the Scots to make the bouncy cores of golf balls!

Cheese Pastry Bites

Talk about melt-in-your-mouth — these flaky tidbits will disappear from the kitchen as soon as they come out of the oven. They serve as a yummy substitute for hard crackers or rolls, and will become fully soft if you put them in a bag or tight container overnight. Save time by using pouches of pre-shredded cheese.

---

1 cup water
¼ cup butter or margarine
1 cup all-purpose flour
4 eggs
1 cup Swiss or Cheddar cheese, grated
½ cup Parmesan cheese, grated

Preheat oven to 400 degrees. Bake for 10 minutes, then turn oven down to 350 degrees and bake an additional 18 minutes.

In a medium saucepan, boil water and butter or margarine until melted together. Remove from heat, let cool for 5 minutes, then stir in flour until completely mixed. Add one egg at a time; the first one will take several minutes to combine, but it will work! Stir in cheeses.

Drop by teaspoonfuls onto greased cookie sheets, 15 to 18 per sheet. Bake at 400 degrees for 10 minutes, then turn oven down to 350 degrees and bake an additional 18 minutes. Makes about 3 dozen "bites."

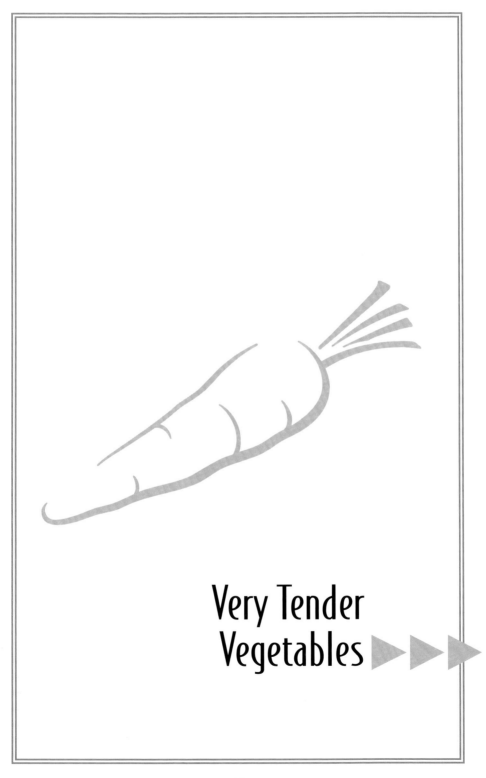

Very Tender Vegetables ▶▶▶

▼ ▼ ▼
Broccoli n' Stuffing Casserole

Frozen chopped broccoli makes this an easy dish to prepare last minute, and you can vary it by using whichever cream soup you happen to have on hand. By baking it in a pot with a lid, the stuffing remains soft and the vegetables steam through to a much-appreciated tenderness.

---

1 (16 oz.) bag frozen chopped broccoli, thawed
2 cups dry bread stuffing (Pepperidge Farm or other
   non-stovetop brand)
1 Tablespoon dried onion
1 (10¾ oz.) can condensed cream of celery soup,
   undiluted
1 cup (4 oz.) shredded mild Cheddar cheese
(optional: 1 (4 oz.) can mushroom pieces, drained)
(optional: 1 (2 oz.) jar chopped pimentos, drained)

Preheat oven to 350 degrees. Bake for 30 minutes.

Grease a 3-quart casserole. In a large mixing bowl, stir together all ingredients, then spoon the mix into the casserole. Cover with a lid or foil. Bake at 350 degrees for 30 minutes. Serves six to eight.

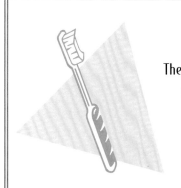

Tooth Trivia...
The Chinese made the first toothbrushes in 1498, using hog bristles. Later versions included horsehair and badger fur, but nothing really worked better for the bristles until the invention of nylon in 1938.

▼ ▼ ▼

Maple Acorn Squash

No need for braces-wearers to feel limited. Add variety to a favorite dinner by serving slices of golden acorn squash, baked to a mellow sweetness with maple syrup. The wonders of the microwave make this cook up quickly, too.

1 or 2 whole acorn squash
¼ to ½ cup maple syrup (pure or the pancake variety)
Water

Preheat oven to 350 degrees. If squash is softened (precooked) in microwave, bake 30 minutes; if not precooked, bake 60 to 75 minutes, depending on size.

Prick the outside skin of the squash three or four times with a fork, to create steam release holes. Place one squash at a time in a microwave oven, and cook on high for ten minutes, turning over once. Use hot mitts for handling!

On a cutting board, with a large knife, carefully cut the squash in half, watching out for steam. Use a large spoon to scoop out the seeds and pulp; throw those away. For large squash, cut each half again to make four slices.

In a 9"x13" pan, place the halves or slices, skin-side down. Pour 2 Tablespoons of maple syrup into each half or slice; it should hold the syrup in. Pour water around the squash to about the half-inch level; this helps steam the slices while they bake.

Place pan on middle rack of oven and bake at 350 degrees, uncovered, for 30 minutes if the squash was precooked in the microwave. Otherwise, check for fork tenderness at 1 hour; thicker squash will take longer. Be careful of the hot water when taking the pan out of the oven — it makes the pan heavy and easily tipped. Each squash serves two to four.

▲▲▲▲▲▲▲▲▲▲▲▲▲▲▲▲▲▲▲▲▲▲▲▲▲▲▲▲▲▲▲▲▲▲▲

▼ ▼ ▼

Squash n' Zucchini Stir Fry

For a zesty change from simple corn, broccoli or green beans, this try-something-different succulent combination produces a flavor that keeps them coming back for more. Call it ratatouille, call it gourmet; you're sure to call it delicious.

———————

1 medium zucchini — peeled, ¼" sliced, each slice
   halved
1 medium yellow squash — peeled, ¼" sliced, each
   slice halved
1 small eggplant — peeled, ¼" sliced, each slice halved
3 small tomatoes (Romas work well) — each cut in
   8 pieces
1 onion, sliced or 1 Tablespoon dried onion
½ teaspoon dried oregano
½ teaspoon dried basil
½ teaspoon dried parsley
¼ cup olive oil (or vegetable oil)

Toss all of the ingredients together, including the oil, in a large no-stick frying pan or a Dutch oven.

Sauté this combination about 20 minutes over medium-high stove heat until everything is tender.

Makes about four servings, as it cooks down considerably.

▼ ▼ ▼

Red Beans and Rice

Sometimes simple is best. When everything else seems too tough to manage, try straightforward red beans and rice, a traditional combination that lends itself to spicing up (add a few drops of hot sauce) or as is for humble satisfaction. Boiling the beans before mixing them with the rice is the key to tender texture.

3½ cups water (total)
1 (15 oz.) can red kidney beans, drained
½ cup onion or 2 Tablespoons dried onion
¾ cup chopped green pepper (or any sweet bell pepper)
¼ teaspoon minced garlic
½ teaspoon dried oregano
½ teaspoon salt
(optional: 2 teaspoons dried basil or 6 crushed basil
    leaves)
1 cup dry long-grained rice

In a large saucepan, combine 1½ cups only of the water with the beans, onion, bell pepper, garlic, and oregano. Bring to a boil, then lower the heat to simmer and cook for 20 minutes.

Add salt, optional basil and the remaining 2 cups of water. Bring to a boil again, then lower the heat to simmer and stir in the rice. Cook for 20 minutes, or to your favorite level of softness. Serves six to eight.

Tooth Trivia...
Model Cindy Crawford, singer Gwen Stefani and actress
Cameron Diaz have all worn braces as adults.

▲▲▲▲▲▲▲▲▲▲▲▲▲▲▲▲▲▲▲▲▲▲▲▲▲▲▲▲▲▲▲▲▲▲▲▲▲▲

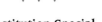

Three-Corn Extravaganza

When you're looking for a change from just cutting the corn off a cob, you'll be pleased with this unusual casserole that serves up soft, almost like a bread stuffing. You can bake it in the oven as described, or in a slow cooker on low to medium for about three hours.

---

1 (1 pound) package frozen corn, thawed
1 (about 14 oz.) can cream-style corn
1 (6 to 8 oz.) package corn muffin mix (dry)
¾ cup water
¼ cup margarine, cut in bits
1 teaspoon salt

Preheat oven to 350 degrees. Bake for 45 minutes.

In a 3-quart casserole dish (or a 3 to 4-quart slow cooker), combine all ingredients and stir together well.

Cover; bake in the oven for 45 minutes at 350 degrees, or about three hours in the slow cooker on low to medium. Serves six to eight.

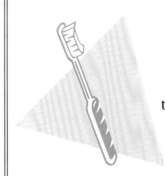

Tooth Trivia...

Levi Spear Parmly (1790–1859), a New Orleans dentist, promoted flossing teeth with silk thread in 1815. The Johnson and Johnson Company of New Brunswick, NJ, was the first company to patent dental floss in 1898.

Definitely Deserved
Desserts ▶▶▶

▼ ▼ ▼
Marvelous Molasses Cookies

This was the very first soft-cookie recipe I collected back in the mid-60s. These molasses marvels melt in your mouth, always stay soft, and have a holiday-festivity aroma that is wonderful even before baking. Yum — the best of gingerbread and ginger snaps in one!

1 cup shortening
1 cup brown sugar, packed
1 egg
½ teaspoon salt
½ cup molasses
½ cup warm water
1 teaspoon baking soda
1 teaspoon ground cinnamon
½ teaspoon ground ginger
2½ cups all-purpose flour

Preheat oven to 350 degrees. Bake for 11 minutes.

In a large bowl, combine shortening, brown sugar, egg, salt and molasses, using an electric mixer and beating until fluffy. Add cinnamon and ginger. In a small bowl or measuring cup, stir the baking soda into the warm water; add water mixture to the molasses mixture alternately with the flour until well blended.

Drop by tablespoons onto greased cookie sheets. Bake for 11 minutes at 350 degrees. Makes about four dozen. Store in a covered container.

▼ ▼ ▼

Sensational Cinnamon Snickerdoodles

Real estate agents tell us that the fragrance of freshly baked cinnamon cookies will make your home irresistible. With this sensationally soft version of the classic cinnamon cookie, even your own guests may not want to leave!

----

1 cup shortening
1½ cups sugar
2 eggs
2¾ cups all-purpose flour
2 teaspoons cream of tartar
1 teaspoon baking soda
½ teaspoon salt
2 Tablespoons sugar
2 teaspoons cinnamon

Preheat oven to 400 degrees. Bake for 8–10 minutes (don't over bake).

In a large bowl, use an electric mixer on low to combine the shortening, 1½ cups sugar and eggs. Add flour, cream of tartar, baking soda and salt. In a separate, small bowl, stir together the 2 Tablespoons of sugar and the cinnamon, to use later.

Chill the dough in the refrigerator for about an hour. With well-floured hands, pinch bits of dough and roll them into 1-inch balls. Roll each ball in the cinnamon sugar until coated.

Bake on ungreased cookie sheets for 8 to 10 minutes at 400 degrees. Makes about five dozen. Store in a covered container.

Fudgy Cocoa Bites

Using cocoa powder instead of melted baking chocolate is one of the secrets to baking soft cookies (another is using shortening instead of margarine or butter). If you're looking for a change from brownies, this is a great melt-in-your-mouth alternative.

----

1 cup shortening
1 cup sugar
2 Tablespoons water
1 teaspoon vanilla
2 eggs
2 cups all-purpose flour
½ cup cocoa
1 teaspoon salt
½ teaspoon baking powder

Preheat oven to 375 degrees. Bake for 9 minutes.

In a large bowl, combine shortening, sugar, water, and vanilla, using an electric mixer and beating until smooth. Add eggs and mix until blended. Mix flour, cocoa, salt and baking powder slowly into shortening mixture, using low then medium speed.

Drop by tablespoons onto ungreased cookie sheets. Bake 9 minutes at 375 degrees. Makes about three dozen. Store in a covered container to keep the softness.

▼ ▼ ▼

Proper Lemon Tea "Cakes"

These little lemon mounds just melt in your mouth; they may disappear before you get the icing on them, but either way, they're heavenly.

1½ teaspoons vinegar
½ cup milk
½ cup margarine, softened
¾ cup sugar
1 egg
1 teaspoon lemon extract
1¾ cups all-purpose flour
1 teaspoon baking powder
¼ teaspoon baking soda
¼ teaspoon salt

Icing:
2 cups confectioner's (powdered) sugar
1 teaspoon lemon extract
3 Tablespoons water

Preheat oven to 350 degrees. Bake for 11 minutes.

In a small bowl, stir the vinegar into the ½ cup milk. In a large bowl, combine the margarine and sugar, using an electric mixer and blending until fluffy. Add egg and lemon extract, mixing well. Stir in the flour, baking powder, baking soda, salt and milk mixture, beating until smooth. Drop by teaspoon onto ungreased cookie sheets. Bake 11 minutes at 350 degrees. They will be very pale on top. Remove from cookie sheets while still warm so they won't stick.

In a small bowl, stir or whisk together the powdered sugar, water and lemon extract. Drizzle icing by teaspoon onto center of each cake while they are still warm. Makes about three dozen. Store in a covered container.

▲▲

▼ ▼ ▼

Jiffy Jam Delights

These cookies taste something like a soft shortbread. They mix and bake very quickly, and look like jewels done with a variety of colorful jams.

½ cup margarine, softened
½ cup sugar
½ teaspoon salt
1 egg
1 teaspoon vanilla
1⅓ cups all-purpose flour

Topping:
Jam of your choice (works better than jelly because it is thicker), about 1 cup — you can use several different jams to make a variety of cookies

Preheat oven to 350 degrees. Bake for 9 minutes.

In a large bowl, combine margarine, sugar, salt, egg and vanilla, using an electric mixer and blending until smooth. Mix in flour.

Drop from tablespoons onto greased cookie sheet. Dip a teaspoon into water and use the backside of the tip to make a dent in the center of each cookie; dip spoon each time in water to keep dough from sticking. Fill each dent with about 1 teaspoon of jam. Bake for 9 minutes at 350 degrees. Makes about two dozen. Store in a covered container.

Tooth Trivia...
In 1848, Milton Waldo Hanchett of Syracuse, NY, patented the dental chair.

▼ ▼ ▼

Peach n' Pear Softies

Fruit plays a delicious role in these out-of-the-ordinary, soft vanilla cookies. I use mixed fruit cocktail for simplicity, but you could cut up canned pears or peaches if you prefer a single fruit flavor.

½ cup raisins (soak in warm water about 15 minutes,
  then drain)
¾ cup sugar
½ cup margarine, softened
2 eggs
½ teaspoon vanilla
2 cups all-purpose flour
1 teaspoon baking powder
½ teaspoon cinnamon
½ cup canned fruit cocktail (drained) or ½ cup cut-up
  canned fruit

Preheat oven to 350 degrees. Bake for 14 minutes.

Soak raisins; drain. In a large bowl, mix the sugar and margarine with an electric mixer until blended. Add eggs and vanilla. Stir in flour, baking powder and cinnamon. With a large spoon, fold in the softened raisins and fruit cocktail.

Drop by tablespoons onto greased cookie sheet. Bake 14 minutes at 350 degrees. Makes about 30 cookies. Store in a covered container.

Tooth Trivia...
You can visit the Dr. Samuel D Harris National Museum of Dentistry, a Smithsonian Affiliate, in Baltimore, MD.

▲▲

▼ ▼ ▼

Quick Cake-Mix Cookies

Everyone has days when fast is best. With this recipe, you can easily convert your favorite cake flavor (German chocolate, spice, lemon, orange, etc.) into soft drop-cookies with a minimum of ingredients.

———————

    1 box cake mix (any flavor, the size that makes two
        9" rounds)
    3 eggs
    ½ cup water
    ½ cup vegetable oil
    ¾ cup all-purpose flour
    ½ teaspoon baking soda

Preheat oven to 350 degrees. Bake for 9 minutes.

In a large bowl, combine all ingredients, using an electric mixer until well blended and creamy (about 1 minute.)

Drop by tablespoons onto a greased cookie sheet. Bake 9 minutes at 350 degrees. Makes about four dozen. Store in a covered container.

Tooth Trivia...
The Colgate company mass-produced pleasantly
scented toothpaste in a jar in 1873.

▲▲

▼ ▼ ▼
Fudge Toppers

A simple swirl of semi-sweet fudgy topping perfectly balances the brown sugar in these soft, feather-light mounds. Thanks to Hilary (Daughter #1) for the inspiration.

½ cup margarine, softened
¾ cup brown sugar, packed
1 egg
1 teaspoon vanilla
1¾ cups all-purpose flour
1 teaspoon baking powder
¼ teaspoon baking soda
¼ teaspoon salt
½ cup milk

Topping:
12 oz. chocolate chips
3 Tablespoons milk

Preheat oven to 350 degrees. Bake for 11 minutes.

In a large bowl, combine the margarine and sugar, using an electric mixer and blending well. Add egg and vanilla, mixing well. Add flour, baking powder, baking soda, salt and milk, beating until soft; batter will be slightly stiff. Drop by teaspoon onto ungreased cookie sheets. Bake 11 minutes at 350 degrees.

In a small saucepan, melt the chocolate bits and the milk, stirring together over low heat until smooth. Use a small spoon or knife to quickly spread a teaspoon of the chocolate topping on each cookie while topping is still warm. Makes about four dozen. Store in a covered container.

Lemon Pudding Yummies

So very moist, these are especially nice for those first few tender days. Serve them with a glass of milk for an afternoon (or midnight!) snack.

¾ cup shortening
½ cup sugar
2 (3¾ oz.) packages of instant lemon pudding (dry)
3 eggs
2 cups all-purpose flour
¾ teaspoon baking soda
¼ teaspoon salt
½ cup milk

Preheat oven to 350 degrees. Bake for 10 minutes.

In a large bowl, combine the shortening, sugar and dry pudding mix, using an electric mixer and blending until creamy. Add eggs and mix thoroughly. Add flour, baking soda, salt and milk, and mix until well blended.

Drop by tablespoons onto greased cookie sheets. Bake 10 minutes at 350 degrees. Makes about four dozen. Store in a covered container.

Tooth Trivia...

In Paris, Pierre Fauchard (1678–1761), wrote the book, The Surgeon Dentist, which has been called the book that made dentistry a profession. It included a chapter on ways to straighten teeth.

▼ ▼ ▼

Lime-Graham Cheesecake Nibbles

Kick-start your taste buds with these tangy lime cheesecakes layered into cupcake papers. The easy crust combines graham-cracker crumbs with melted margarine, and the fluffy filling gets its zip from real lime juice. For an even "spicier" version, substitute finely crushed gingersnaps for the grahams.

Crust:

  $1\frac{1}{2}$ cups graham-cracker crumbs (about 9 double-square crackers, crushed)

  3 Tablespoons margarine, melted

– or –

  $1\frac{1}{2}$ cups gingersnap crumbs (about 24 to 30 gingersnap cookies, crushed)

  3 Tablespoons margarine, melted

Filling:

  2 eggs, separated

  $\frac{1}{8}$ teaspoon salt

  2 (8 oz.) packages cream cheese, softened

  $\frac{3}{4}$ cup sugar

  3 drops green food coloring

  2 Tablespoons lime juice

  1 Tablespoon all-purpose flour

Preheat oven to 325 degrees. Bake for 25 minutes.

Line two muffin tins with 24 cupcake papers. In a medium bowl, stir together the crumbs and margarine. Spoon 1 Tablespoon of the crumb mixture into each paper. Press down the mixture firmly with the bottom of a small juice glass.

In a medium bowl, using an electric mixer, beat together the egg whites and the salt until the mixture forms soft peaks. Set aside. In a large bowl, use the mixer to beat together the cream cheese, sugar, food coloring, lime juice and flour, until fluffy. Add the yolks until well mixed, then use a spoon to fold in the whites.

Spoon a heaping tablespoon of the lime mixture into each paper. Bake at 325 degrees for 25 minutes. Cool on the counter for 20 minutes, then keep refrigerated. Makes two dozen.

▼ ▼ ▼

Butterscotch Brownies

My mother started making these "non-chocolate" brownies when I was a little girl. Since she in turn has lived with our family since our oldest daughter was one, our girls have renamed them "Grandma's Tannies." By any name, they're fabulous, and a delightful change from the traditional chocolate version.

⅓ cup vegetable oil
2 cups brown sugar, packed
2 eggs
1½ cups all-purpose flour
2 teaspoons baking powder
1 teaspoon salt
1 teaspoon vanilla
(optional: 1 cup butterscotch bits)

Preheat oven to 350 degrees. Bake for 40 minutes.

In a large bowl, combine oil and brown sugar, using an electric mixer and blending well. Add eggs. Stir in flour, baking powder and salt, then add vanilla.

Spread batter into a greased 9"x9" pan. If desired, sprinkle 1 cup butterscotch bits over top. Bake 40 minutes at 350 degrees. After cooling one minute, swirl the bits with a knife to give a marbleized effect.

To keep brownies soft, cover pan with foil while still hot, or cut the brownies in squares and store them in a covered container. Makes two dozen.

Tooth Trivia...

In the 17th and early 18th centuries, French dentists encouraged people to brush their teeth.

▼ ▼ ▼
Molasses Raisin Bars

My mother experimented for years to create these warm treats as a tribute to those found in both our local grocery store and wonderful, tiny, small town French bakery. Don't be put off by the number of spices — line them up on your counter and they'll go in quickly. The aroma of these bars while baking makes me think of holidays, but I love them all year 'round.

---

1 cup raisins (soak 5 minutes in warm water, then
    drain)
1 cup shortening
1 cup brown sugar, packed
½ cup white sugar
½ cup molasses
2 eggs
3 cups all-purpose flour
1 teaspoon baking soda
1 teaspoon cinnamon
½ teaspoon nutmeg
½ teaspoon ginger
(optional: ½ teaspoon cloves)
½ teaspoon salt
½ cup water

Preheat oven to 350 degrees. Bake for 20 minutes.

Soak raisins; drain. In a large bowl, combine shortening, brown sugar and white sugar, using an electric mixer and blending until smooth. Add molasses and eggs. In a medium-sized bowl, stir together flour, baking soda, cinnamon, nutmeg, ginger, optional cloves and salt. Add flour mixture to shortening mixture alternately with water. Stir in raisins with a large spoon.

Use a spatula to spread batter in a greased and floured 11"x17" cookie sheet. Bake for 20 minutes at 350 degrees. Makes about 30 bars.

▼▼▼
Fudgy Zucchini Zoom-Bars

Health and heaven combined, or at least it seems so. My family loves the slightly bittersweet flavor (you might want to add ¼ cup more sugar), and what a great way to get some vegetables into a snack. No chocolate-lover will know that zucchini is the secret ingredient!

————————————

2 cups all-purpose flour
1¼ cups sugar
1½ teaspoons baking soda
1 teaspoon salt
⅓ cup cocoa powder
2 cups finely grated zucchini
¼ cup vegetable oil
2 teaspoons vanilla

Preheat oven to 350 degrees. Bake for 25 minutes.

In a medium-sized bowl, using a spoon or whisk, combine the flour, sugar, baking soda, salt and cocoa. In a large bowl, stir together the zucchini, oil and vanilla. Add the dry ingredients to the zucchini mixture and stir together until well mixed and glossy.

Grease or oil a 9"x13" pan. Pour in batter. Bake at 350 degrees for 25 minutes. Makes two dozen.

Hint: I try to keep some zucchini grated and divided in 2-cup plastic bags in my freezer to thaw for making quick treats like these.

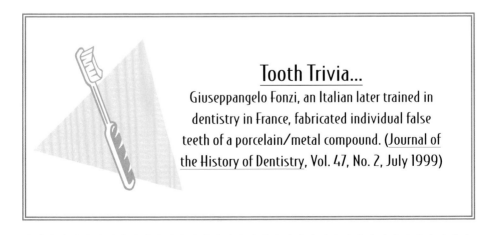

Tooth Trivia...
Giuseppangelo Fonzi, an Italian later trained in dentistry in France, fabricated individual false teeth of a porcelain/metal compound. (Journal of the History of Dentistry, Vol. 47, No. 2, July 1999)

▼ ▼ ▼

Mint-Cheesecake Cocoa Bars

With a blush of mint sandwiched between two types of chocolate layers, these beautiful squares elevate brownies to a royal reward. They're worth the extra time — keep them in mind for days when you really deserve a treat, or you want to make an impression for a party.

_____

Chocolate Base:
> 1¾ cups sugar
> 3 eggs
> 2 teaspoons vanilla
> 1 cup all-purpose flour
> 7 Tablespoons margarine
> 4 (1 oz.) squares of baking (unsweetened) chocolate

Mint Cream Layer:
> 1 (8 oz.) package cream cheese, softened
> 1 Tablespoon margarine
> 1 Tablespoon cornstarch
> 1 (14 oz.) can condensed milk
> 1 teaspoon mint extract
> 2 drops green food coloring

Chocolate Icing:
> 1 cup (6 oz.) chocolate chips
> ½ cup light cream

Preheat oven to 350 degrees. Total baking time is 37 minutes, in two parts.

Chocolate Base: In a large bowl, using an electric mixer, combine sugar, eggs, vanilla and flour. In a small saucepan, melt 7 Tablespoons of the margarine with the squares of chocolate, stirring until well mixed. Add the chocolate mixture to the sugar mixture and stir well. Grease a 9"x13" pan. Pour the batter into the pan and bake at 350 degrees for 12 minutes. Let cool while making the mint layer.

Mint Cream Layer: In a medium-sized bowl, with an electric mixer, combine the cream cheese, 1 Tablespoon of margarine, and cornstarch. Add the condensed milk, mint extract and food coloring until the mixture is smooth and creamy. Pour over cooled chocolate base and bake at 350 degrees for 25 minutes.

Chocolate Icing: In a small saucepan, mix and melt the chocolate chips and the light cream until slightly thickened. Spread over top of bars. Allow to cool for easier cutting. Very rich tasting — serve in small portions! Makes about four dozen.

▲▲▲▲▲▲▲▲▲▲▲▲▲▲▲▲▲▲▲▲▲▲▲▲▲▲▲▲▲▲▲▲▲▲▲▲▲

▼ ▼ ▼

Mocha Swirl Brownies

For the coffee lover, this is a quick treat that tastes elaborate. When you use a knife to swirl the mocha topping over the brownie base, use an "up and over" motion for an elegant, through-and-through marbleized effect.

Base:
> 1 large (20 to 23 ounce) package brownie mix
> As called for in the mix:
>> Eggs
>> Vegetable oil
>> Water

Topping:
> 1 (8 oz.) package cream cheese, softened
> $\frac{1}{3}$ cup sugar
> 1 egg
> $1\frac{1}{2}$ teaspoons instant coffee granules
> 1 teaspoon vanilla

Preheat oven to 350 degrees. Bake for 35 to 38 minutes.

In a large bowl, stir together the brownie mix according to the package directions. Grease a 9"x13" pan and pour in the brownie batter. Set pan aside.

In a small bowl, with an electric mixer, combine the cream cheese, sugar, 1 egg, coffee granules and vanilla. Beat until thoroughly mixed, though bits of cheese will still show. Spoon the topping onto the unbaked brownie batter. Use a knife to swirl the topping over and partly into the brownie batter, just so you see a nice half-mixed effect.

Bake at 350 degrees for 35 to 38 minutes, so the topping is thoroughly set. Makes two dozen.

▲▲▲▲▲▲▲▲▲▲▲▲▲▲▲▲▲▲▲▲▲▲▲▲▲▲▲▲▲▲▲▲▲▲▲▲▲

Substitution Special:
If you like fruit snacks, you'll love...

Fruity Cut-Outs

Fruit snacks, fruit "leather," gummy bears — whatever your favorite, these smooth and soft fruit shape substitutions will satisfy your craving while keeping braces-hardware safe. Experiment with different fruit flavors to find your own special combination.

---

    1 (6-oz.) (8 serving) package cherry gelatin (dry)
    1 (6-oz.) (8 serving) package raspberry gelatin (dry)
    1½ cups water
    1 cup cranberry-grape juice
    1 teaspoon lemon juice

Empty both packages of dry gelatin powder into a large bowl. In a medium saucepan, stir together the water and juice; bring to a full boil then remove pan from heat.

Pour hot juice mixture slowly into bowl, stirring constantly with a large spoon. Keep stirring for two minutes or until all granules have dissolved. Add lemon juice and stir to mix.

Pour mixture into a 9"x13" pan and place pan in refrigerator. Chill for at least 3 hours or until firm.

Cut into squares with a knife, or into shapes with cookie cutters dipped in hot water. If pieces are hard to get out, set the entire pan for a minute onto a cookie sheet filled with a quarter-inch of hot water. Makes two dozen squares.

Tooth Trivia...

Lingual braces are attached to the back (lingual or tongue side) of the teeth.

▼ ▼ ▼

Soft Ginger Shapes

Who needs to wait for a holiday for the fun of cutting out and decorating gingerbread cookies? They're just as good hot and simple from the oven, but this recipe is special because, with a little care, they do not harden when cooled.

½ cup sugar
½ cup shortening
½ cup molasses
¼ cup water
¾ teaspoon salt
½ teaspoon baking soda
¾ teaspoon ginger
¼ teaspoon nutmeg
2½ cups all-purpose flour
Extra flour (about ¼ cup) for rolling and cutting
Rolling pin and cookie cutters
(optional: prepared frosting)

Preheat oven to 375 degrees. Bake for 8 to 10 minutes.

In a large bowl, combine sugar, shortening, molasses and water, using an electric mixer and beating until creamy. Mix in salt, baking soda, ginger, nutmeg and flour; dough will be stiff. Divide the dough into two mounds, wrap each in waxed paper or sealed containers, and chill them for at least one hour.

Set up a smooth, clean surface (counter or cutting board) and dust it with flour. Put one of the chilled dough mounds in the center, and sprinkle it with more flour. Use a rolling pin to roll out the dough until it is about ¼-inch thick, then cut out shapes with cookie cutters. Be sure to roll out and reuse the scraps until all the dough has been shaped.

Slide cookies onto an ungreased cookie sheet. Bake for 7 minutes at 375 degrees. If desired, decorate the cookies with frosting. Store in covered container. If they start to harden up, place a fresh slice of bread in the container and reseal it.

▲▲

Peanut Butter Kiss Cookies

¾ cup shortening
¾ cup peanut butter
1 cup brown sugar, packed
2 eggs
½ teaspoon salt
½ teaspoon vanilla
½ cup warm water
1 teaspoon baking soda
2½ cups all-purpose flour
about 50 Hershey's chocolate Kisses

Preheat oven to 350 degrees. Bake for 11 minutes.

In a large bowl, combine shortening, peanut butter, and brown sugar, using an electric mixer. Add eggs, salt and vanilla and beat until creamy. In a small bowl or measuring cup, stir the baking soda into the warm water; add water mixture to the peanut butter mixture alternately with the flour until well blended.

Drop by tablespoons onto greased cookie sheets. Bake for 11 minutes at 350 degrees. While they are baking, unwrap the foil from the Kisses. As soon as the cookies come out of the oven, "kiss" them. Makes four dozen. Store in a covered container.

Variation: For a double-chocolate effect, decrease the flour to 2¼ cups, and add ¼ cup cocoa.

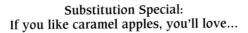

Caramel Apple Dips

Here is the recipe that inspired this book. Brenda longed for a good ol' caramel-dipped apple, but knew that biting into that chewy concoction wasn't exactly the best thing for her braces. It didn't take long for her to figure out this simple substitution, and it won't take you long to fix it, either.

Your favorite apples, washed
Jar of caramel topping/sauce (usually sold in the ice
    cream section)

Core and peel the apples, slice them thinly, and arrange them on a serving plate. Warm the jar of caramel sauce in a microwave, or by setting it in a pan of very hot water. Spoon a bit of the caramel sauce into a small bowl for each person. Pick up an apple slice, dip it in, and enjoy!

Tooth Trivia...

In 14th century Japan, the Buddhist priestess Nakaoka Tei, known as Hotokehime, or Lady of Buddha, constructed an entire set of teeth for herself. This beautifully carved piece of cherry wood is on display in the Tokyo Museum as a discrete witness of the abilities and knowledge of this notable woman. (Journal of the History of Dentistry, Vol. 49, No. 1, March 2001)

▼▼▼
Websites of Interest

www.BracesCookbook.com
Visit for updates. Order **The Braces Cookbook** for friends!

www.ada.org/public/topics/braces_faq.asp
Presented by the American Dental Association, this website provides a serious and informative discussion about braces and orthodontics.

www.agd.org/consumer/topics
The website of the Academy of General Dentistry, with helpful information particularly for adult braces-wearers. Visit both the Adult Braces and the Orthodontics sections.

www.ArchWired.com
An extensive and very current source of information primarily for adults with braces, but with articles, links, and resource pointers interesting for all ages (as well as for parents of children with braces).

www.braces.org
The consumer-oriented website of the American Association of Orthodontists. Great section of Frequently Asked Questions when you visit the About Orthodontics pages.

www.dentaltown.com
An international e-zine and dental community with professional discussion boards covering more than 86 topics, including orthodontics. Anyone can join and ask questions.

www.familytlc.net/smiling_braces_teens.html
Tips on life with braces, especially for teens.

www.pbhs.com/ortho/braces/braces.html
A fun site where you can see how different color combinations will look when you choose new elastics.

www.saveyoursmile.com/parents/dbraces.html
Good general information for parents.

▼▼▼
About the Authors

Pamela Waterman is an author, editor and engineer whose three children had braces in some form for more than seven years. She herself had five years of orthodontic work as a teen, and more recently had a year of adult braces to "make a few adjustments."

Ms. Waterman's books include *The Braces Cookbook 2: Comfort Food with a Gourmet Touch, The Absolute Best Play Days: From Airplanes to Zoos (and Everything In Between)* and *JumpStart 5th Grade Activities.*

Her articles on parenting, craft projects, small business, and home renovation have appeared in such publications as *Family Fun, Cricket, Highlights,* and *Better Homes and Gardens Kids' Rooms.*

Brenda Waterman, now 15, was eleven years old when she created the concept of **The Braces Cookbook.** Comfortably at home in the kitchen as well as at the drawing-board, she has come up with many of the approaches for the innovative "Substitution Specials" recipes and is always thinking of better ways to do things. She completed three phases of orthodontic treatment, can tell you all about Temporary Anchor Devices, and is a pro at mixing "Be-Nice-to-Me Beverages" for herself and her two older braces-veteran sisters. Ms. Waterman enjoys experimenting in the kitchen and preparing meals with an international flair.

▼▼▼

Index

▲▲

▼ ▼ ▼

▲▲▲

▼ ▼ ▼

Give the gift of Comfort-Food Eating to family, friends and patients

ORDER HERE

YES, please send me more copies of *The Braces Cookbook*

1 copy	($9.95 plus s/h $3.50)	$13.45
2 copies	($19.90 plus s/h $5.00)	$24.90
3 copies	($29.85 plus s/h $7.00)	$36.85

And for 50 more great tender-teeth recipes, try:
The Braces Cookbook 2: Comfort Food with a Gourmet Touch

1 copy	($14.95 plus s/h $3.50)	$18.45
2 copies	($29.90 plus s/h $5.00)	$34.90
3 copies	($44.85 plus s/h $7.00)	$51.85

A great gift for a new braces-wearer is one of each title:
1 copy each, *The Braces Cookbook* and *The Braces Cookbook 2*
($24.90 plus s/h $5.00)) $29.90

(Arizona residents please add $0.75 sales tax per book).
For Canada and other countries, please phone us for shipping costs.

Orthodontists: Call us for professional discount quantity pricing, at 480-897-3380, or view our website at www.BracesCookbook.com.

Make check out to: The Discovery Box.

☐ My check or money order for $_____is enclosed.

Name_____

Organization _____

Address_____

City/State/Zip_____

Phone_____ Email (optional) _____

Mail to: Braces Cookbook Request

The Discovery Box
1955 W. Baseline Rd.
Ste. 113-234
Mesa AZ 85202

Any questions? Call us at 480-897-3380

www.BracesCookbook.com

▲▲

▼▼▼

The Braces Cookbook

can be a valuable part
of your Non-Profit group efforts!

Contact us for more information about how we can work
together with bulk orders
at a discount.

Call 480-897-3380
or send email to:
thediscoverybox@earthlink.net

▲▲▲

▼▼▼
Your Turn

**Have a tip, easy-eating idea, or recipe
you'd share with us about life with braces?**

**Want to let us know what you think about
*The Braces Cookbook?***

Write it down here and mail this page to us at:

The Discovery Box
1955 W. Baseline Rd.
Ste. 113-234
Mesa, AZ 85202

Or, email us at: *thediscoverybox@earthlink.net*

We'd love to hear from you!

_____

_____

_____

_____

_____

_____

Your Name_____

Address _____

_____

Age of the braces-wearer(s)_____

Optional: Phone Number_____

Optional: Email address _____

▲▲▲▲▲▲▲▲▲▲▲▲▲▲▲▲▲▲▲▲▲▲▲▲▲▲▲▲▲▲▲▲▲▲▲▲▲▲▲

Notes

▼▼▼
Notes

▲▲▲